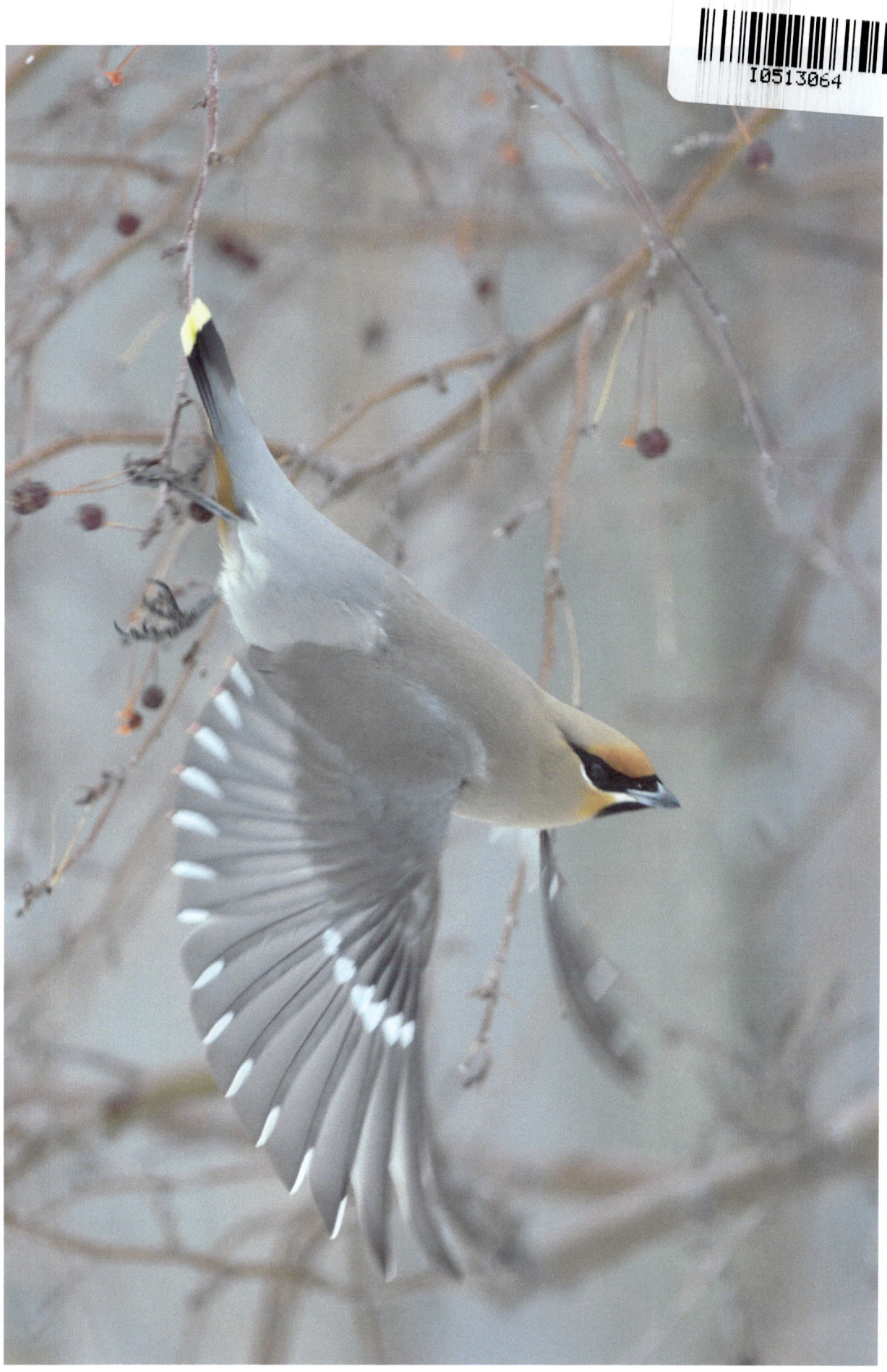

THE
BEAUTY OF
BOHEMIAN WAXWINGS

BY

Pervaiz Iqbal

© Copyright 2023 by Printed Page Publishers - All rights reserved.

It is not legal to reproduce, duplicate, or transmit any part of this document in either electronic means or printed format. Recording of this publication is strictly prohibited.

This book is dedicated to: My Father Faiz Ali

Introduction

This book was long overdue. Many friends in person and on Facebook were asking me to publish something that contained the photographs the I took on regular basis. There were many options to work on or to start from somewhere.

Bohemian waxwings always inspire me because of their elegant beauty and photogenic qualities. My admiration for them and camera in hands even in minus 30C is a precursor in shaping of this book.

This book is a photo book, an album just like any other album e.g wedding album that contain different poses of Bohemian waxwing in different styles.

I hope you will enjoy this book and this encouragement will probably motivate me to put another book on the market.

I am not a professional photographer but a hobbyist. That loves the outdoors and nature.

This book will give the reader a chance to admire this beautiful bird and nature for the reader.

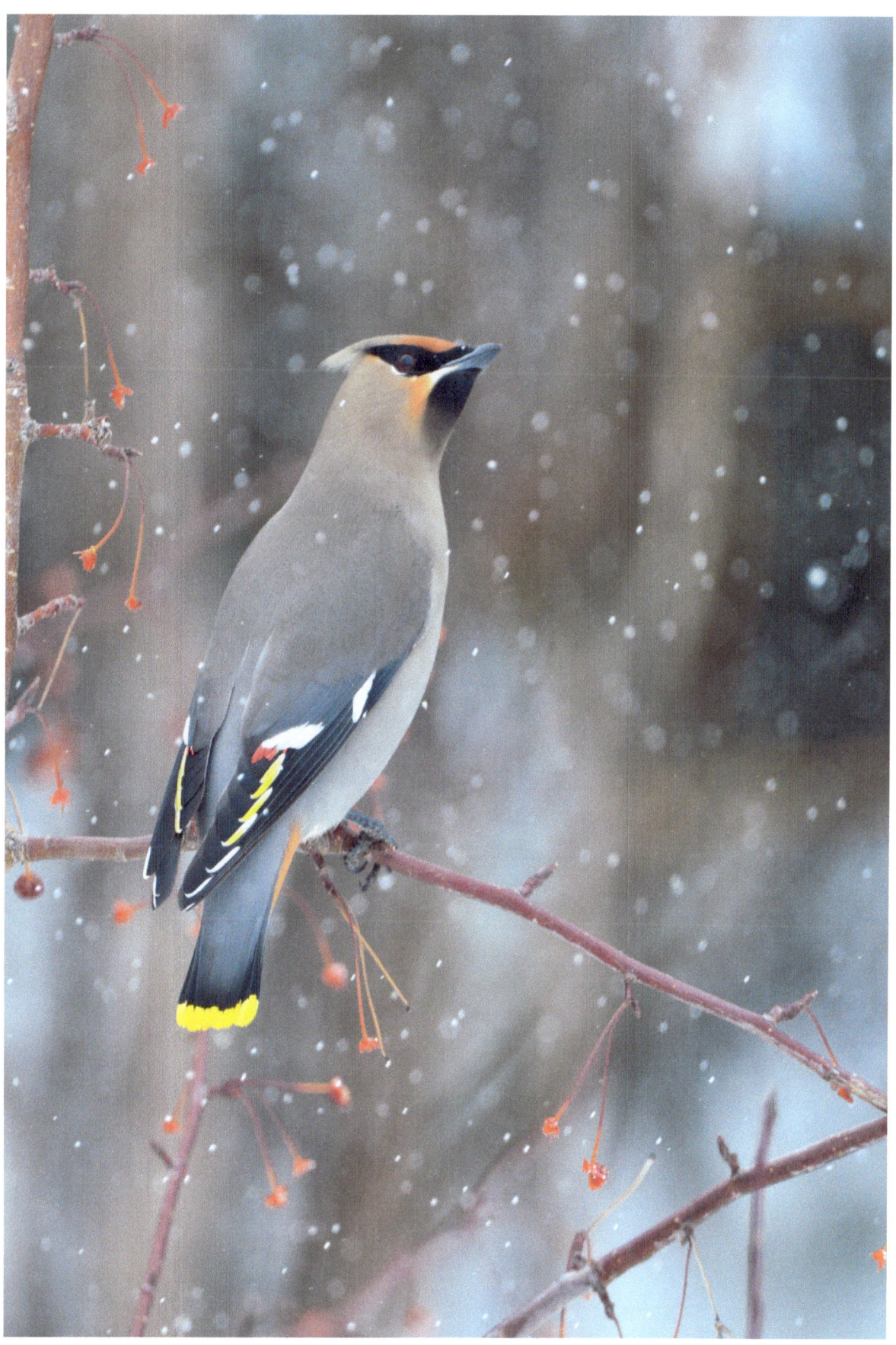

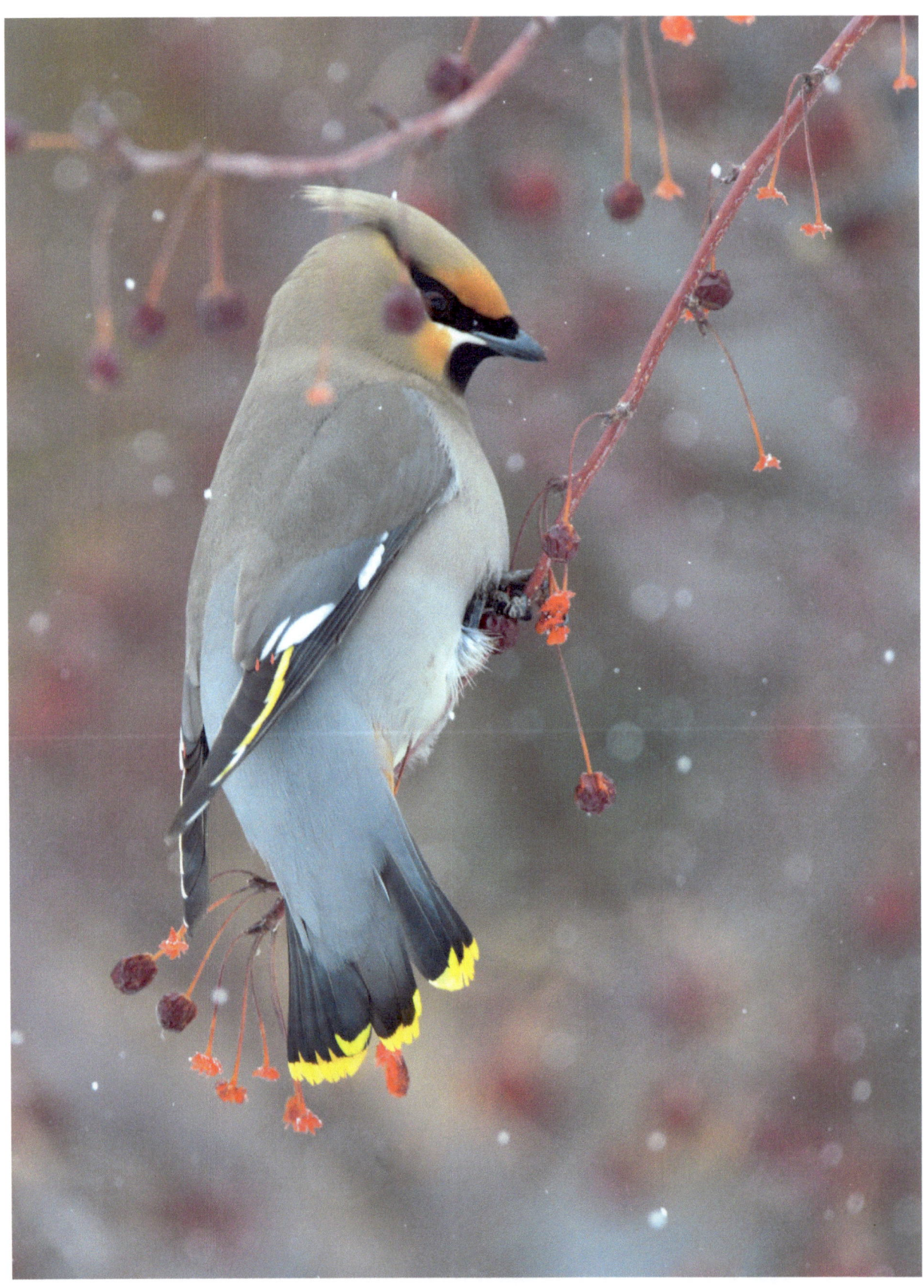

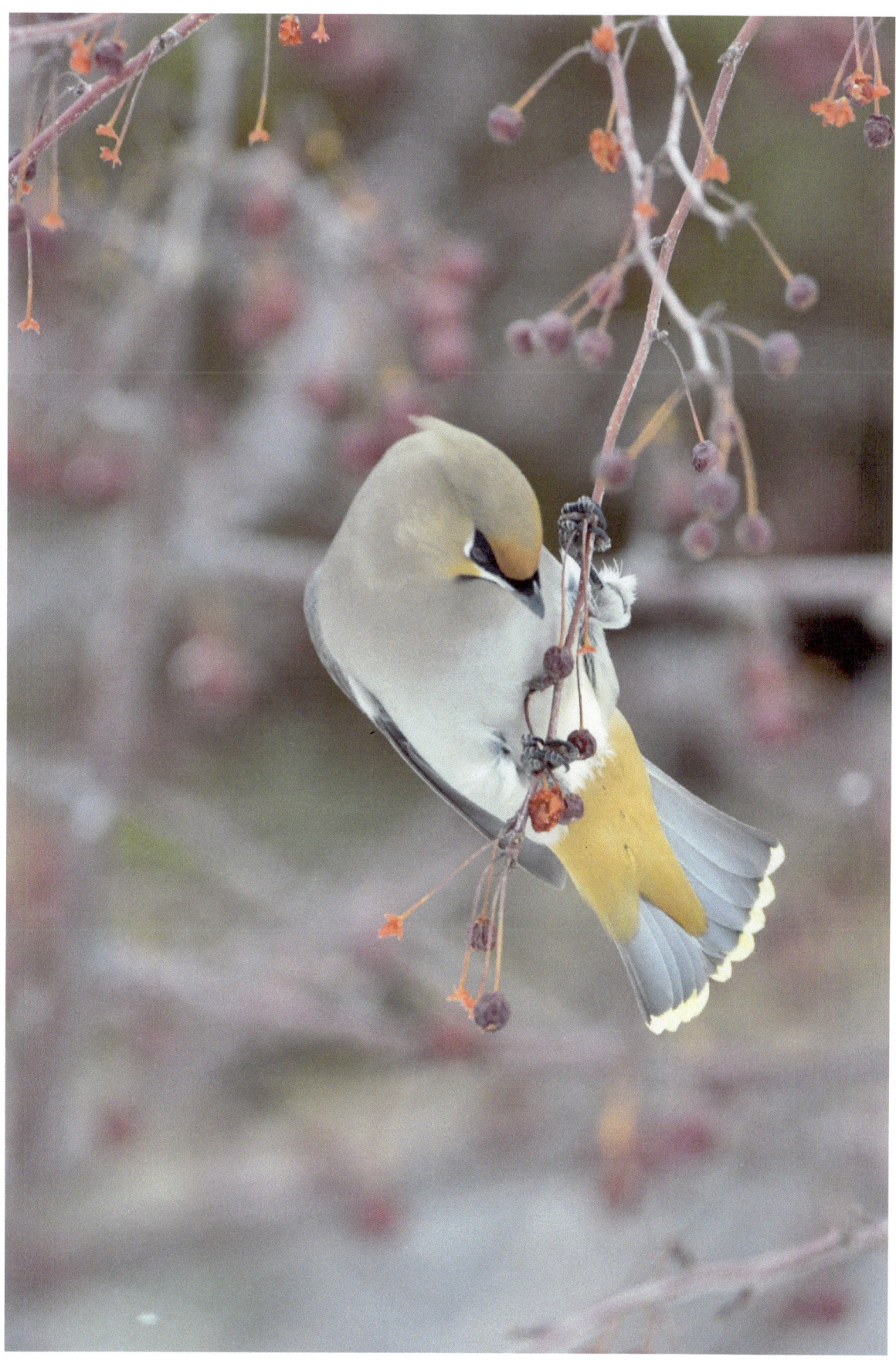

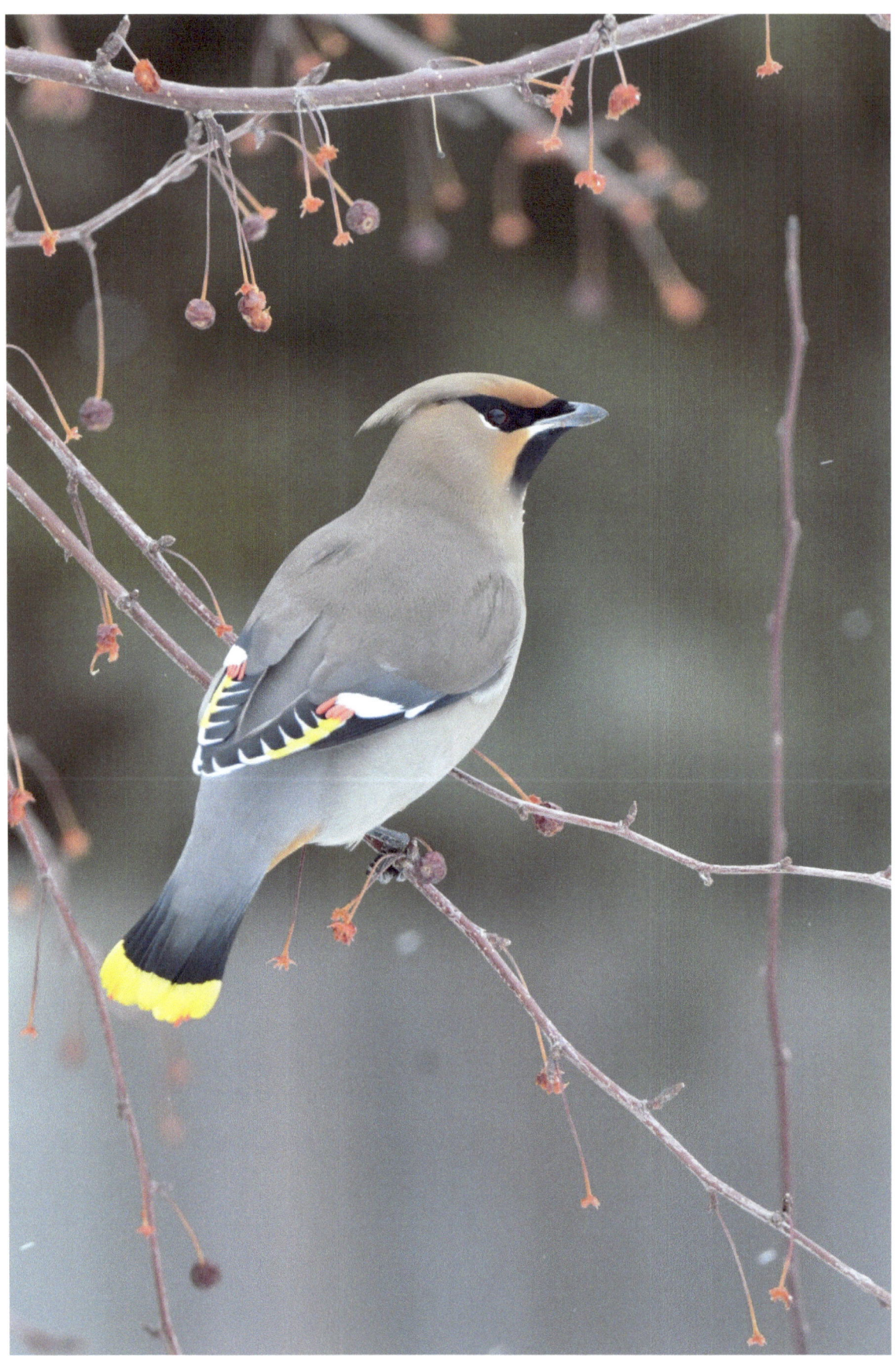

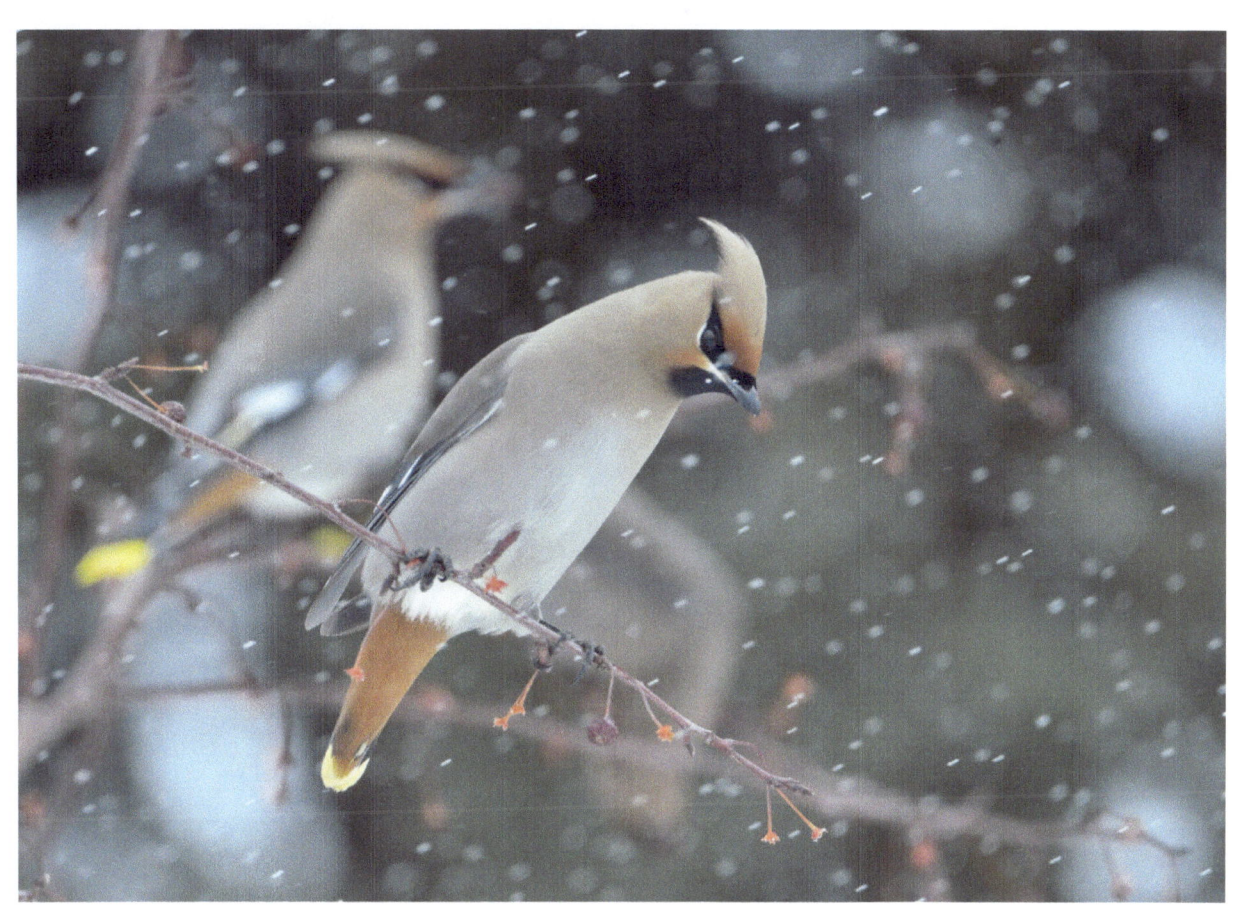

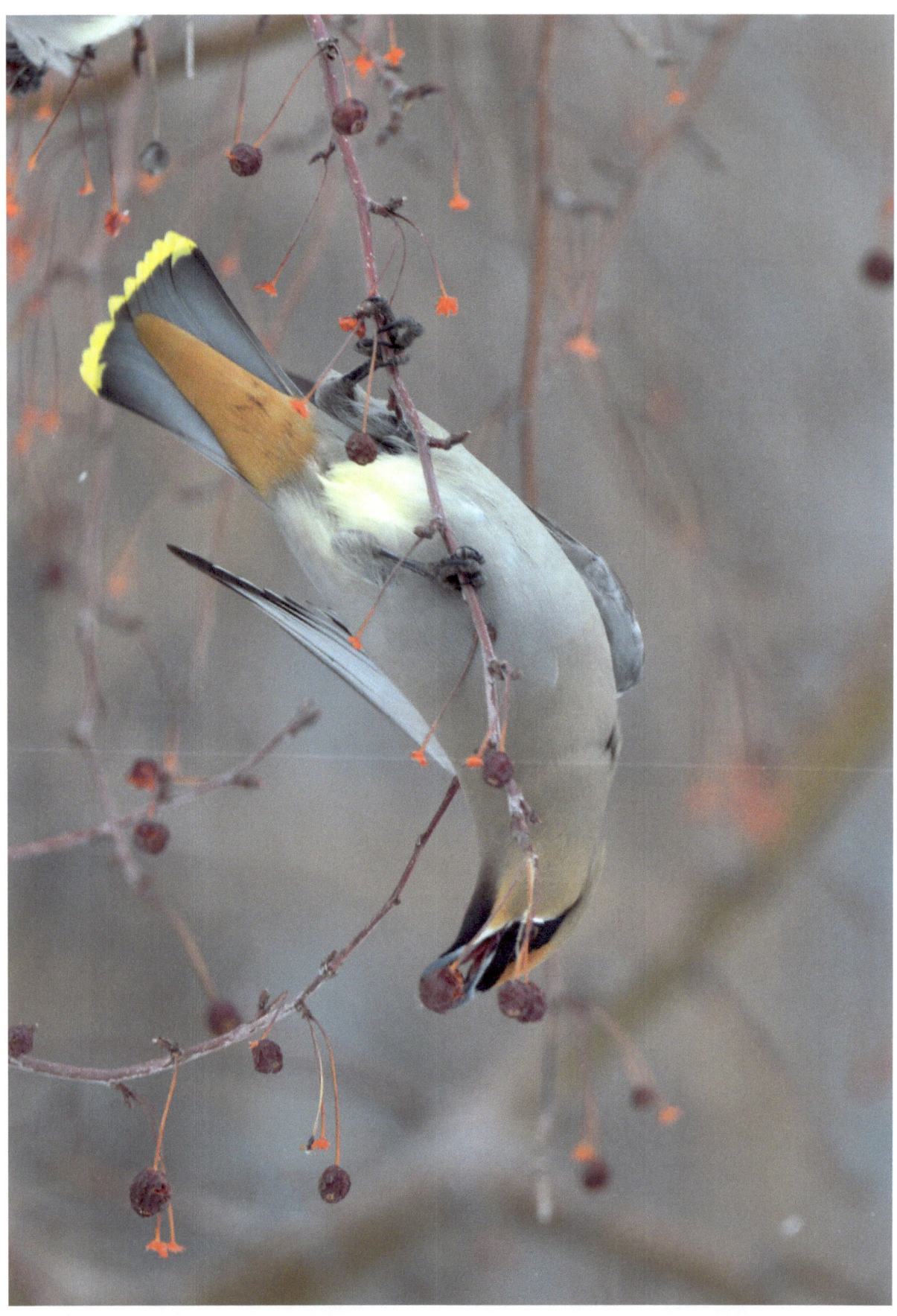

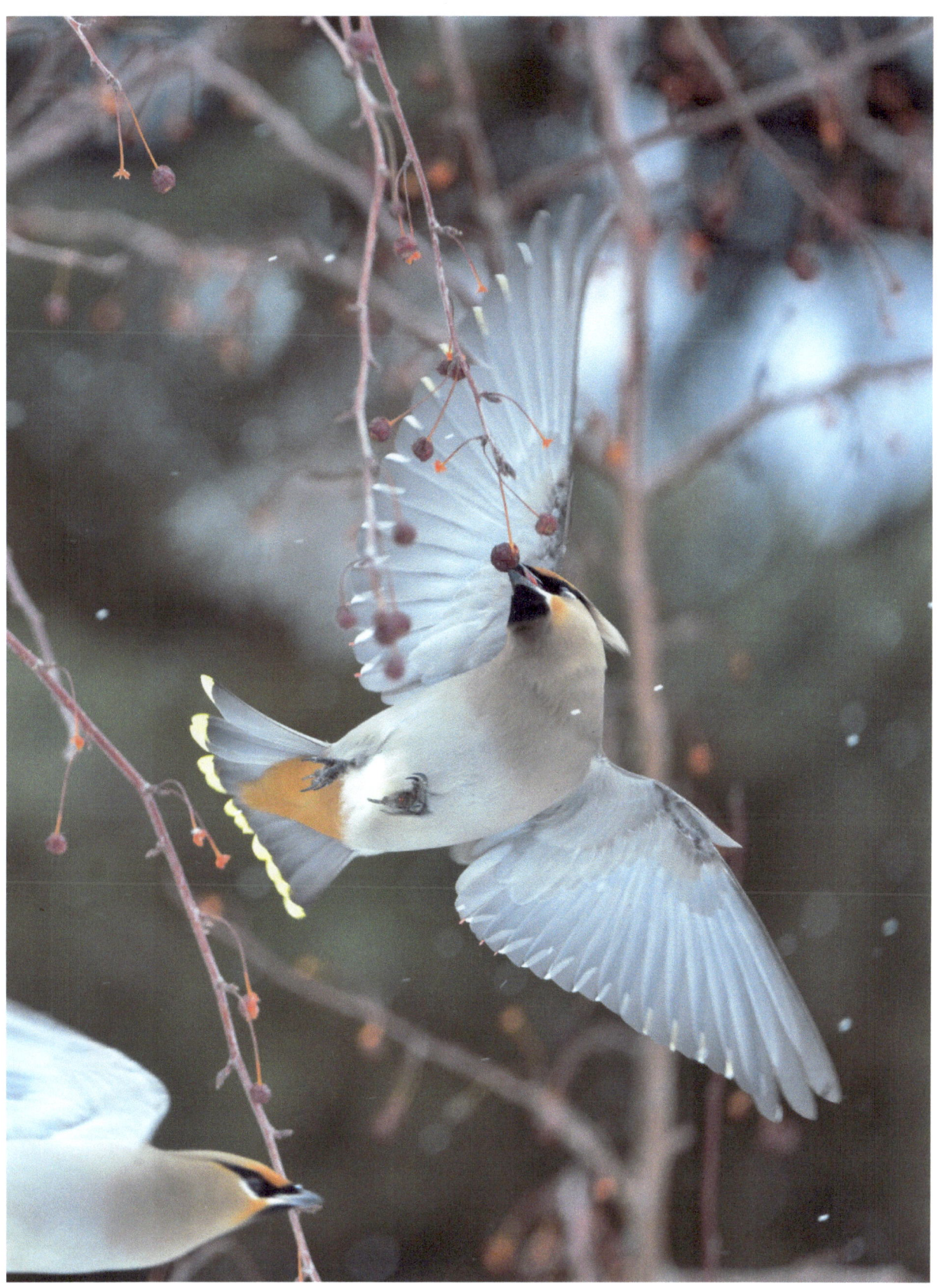

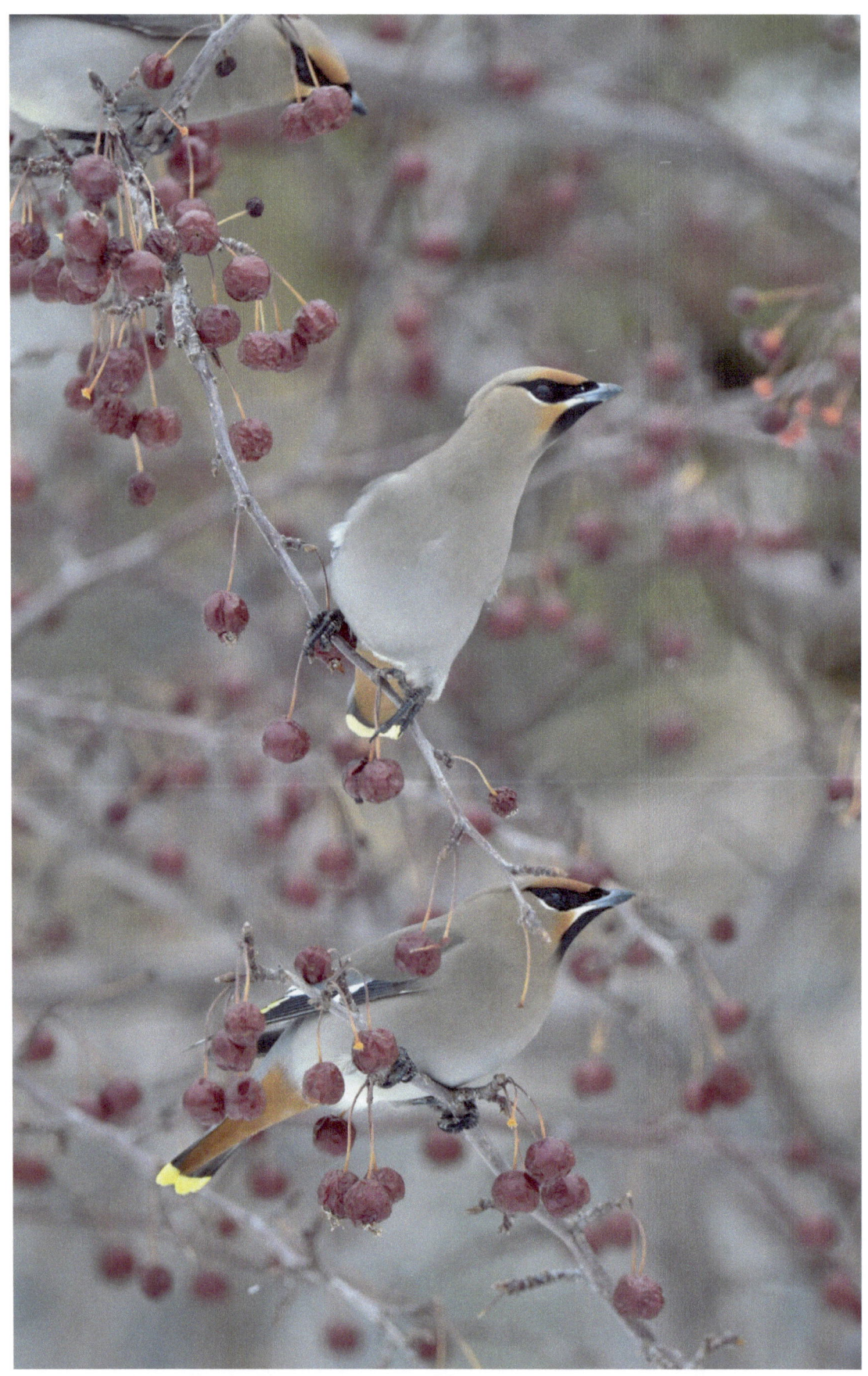

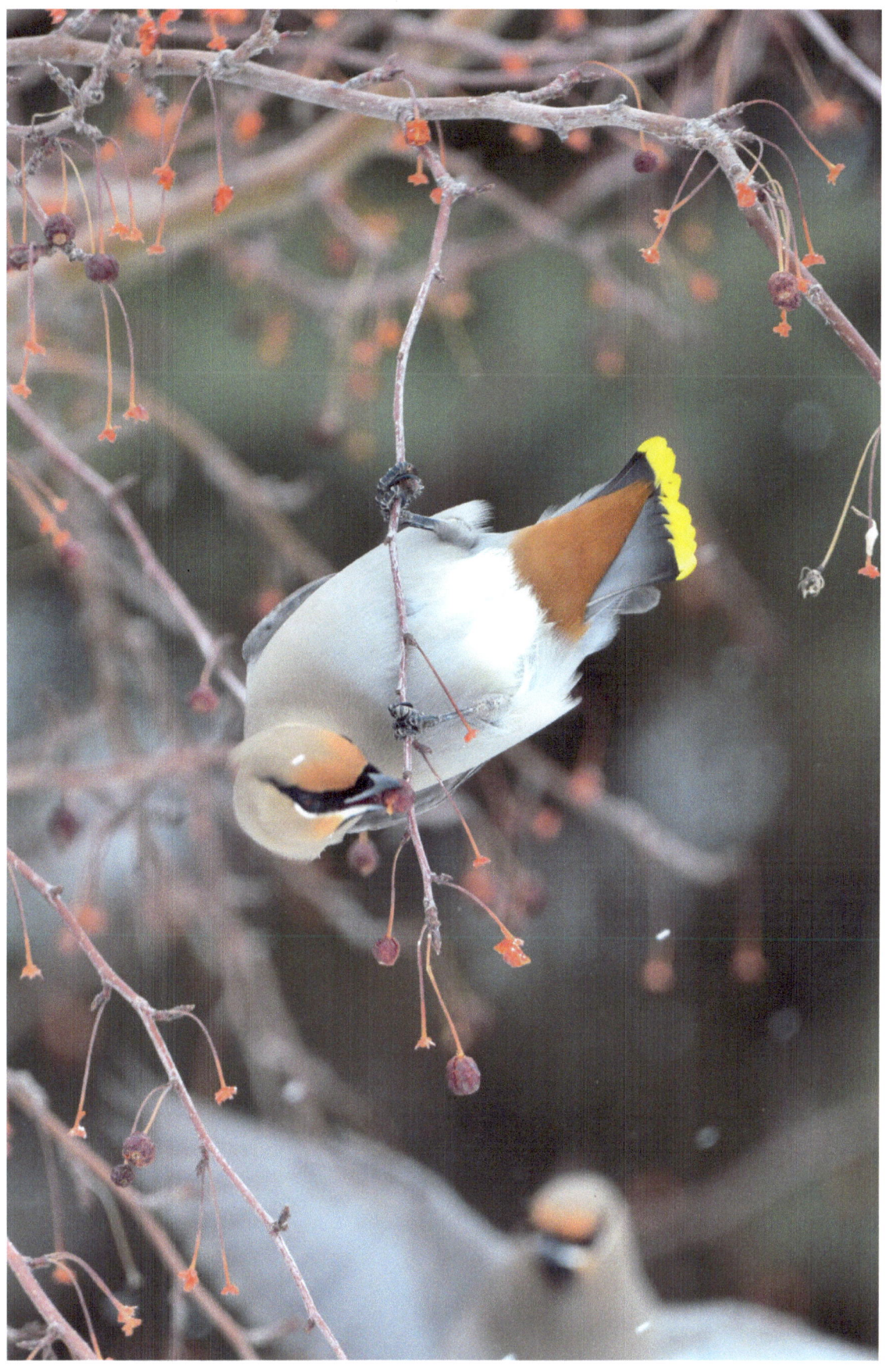

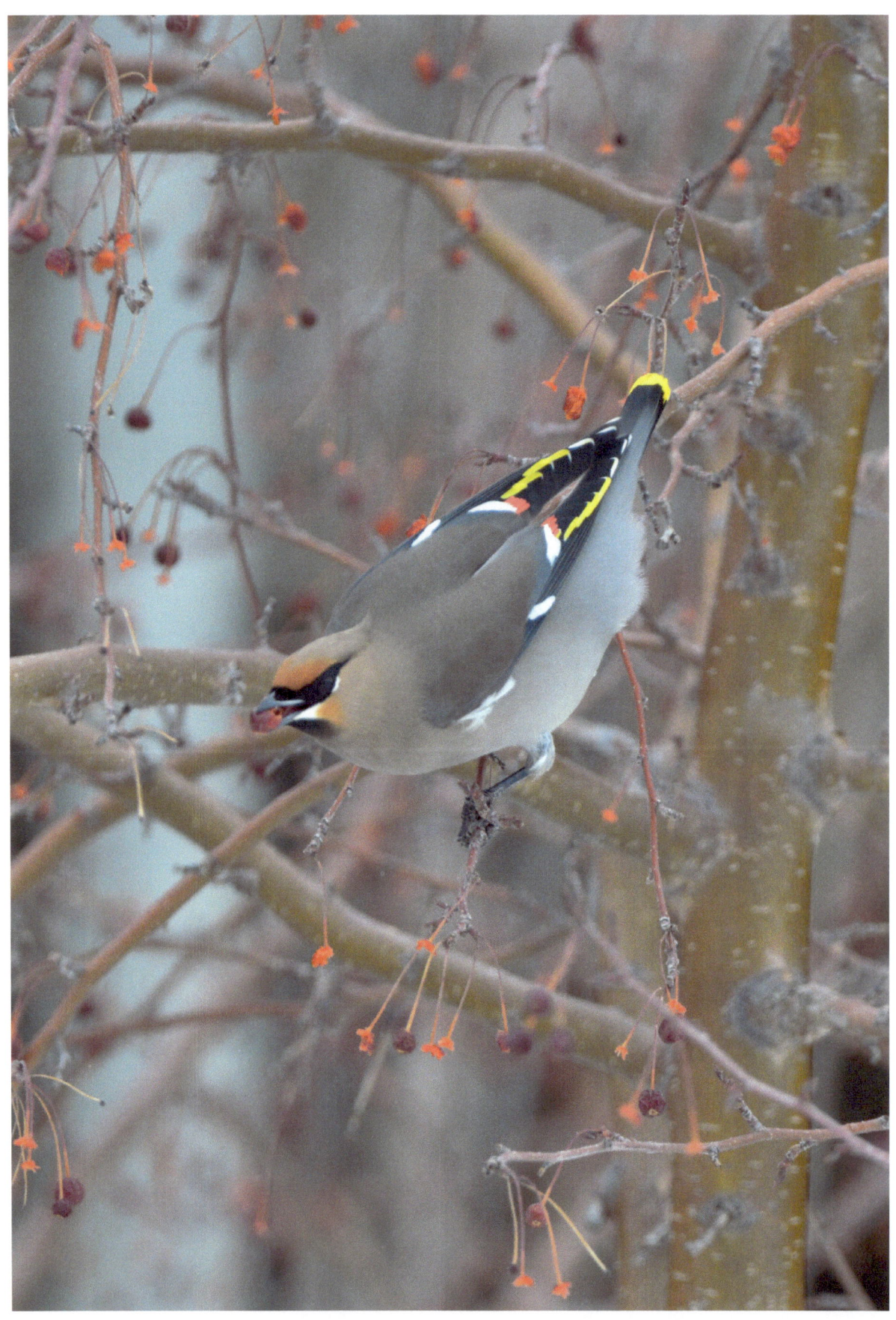

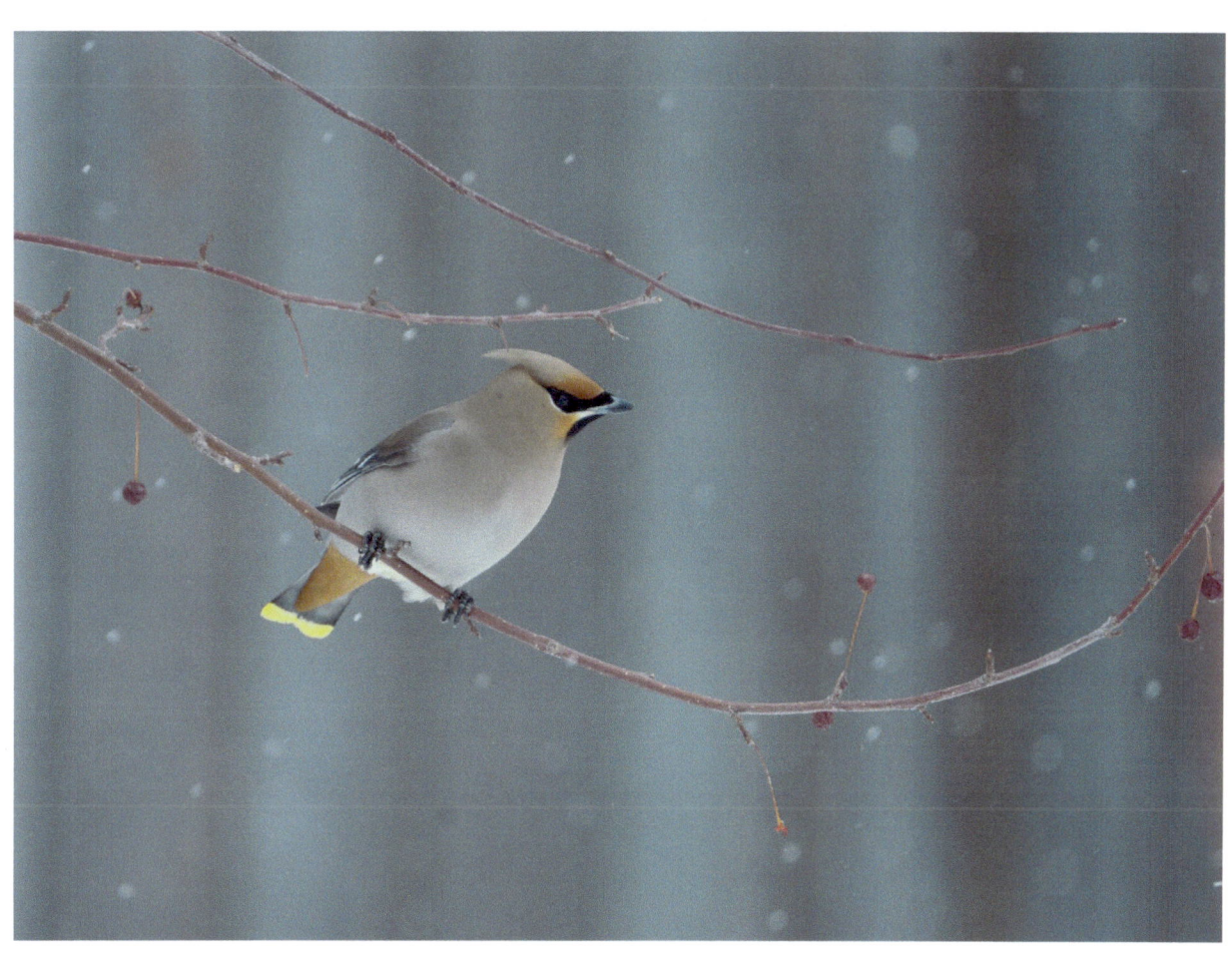

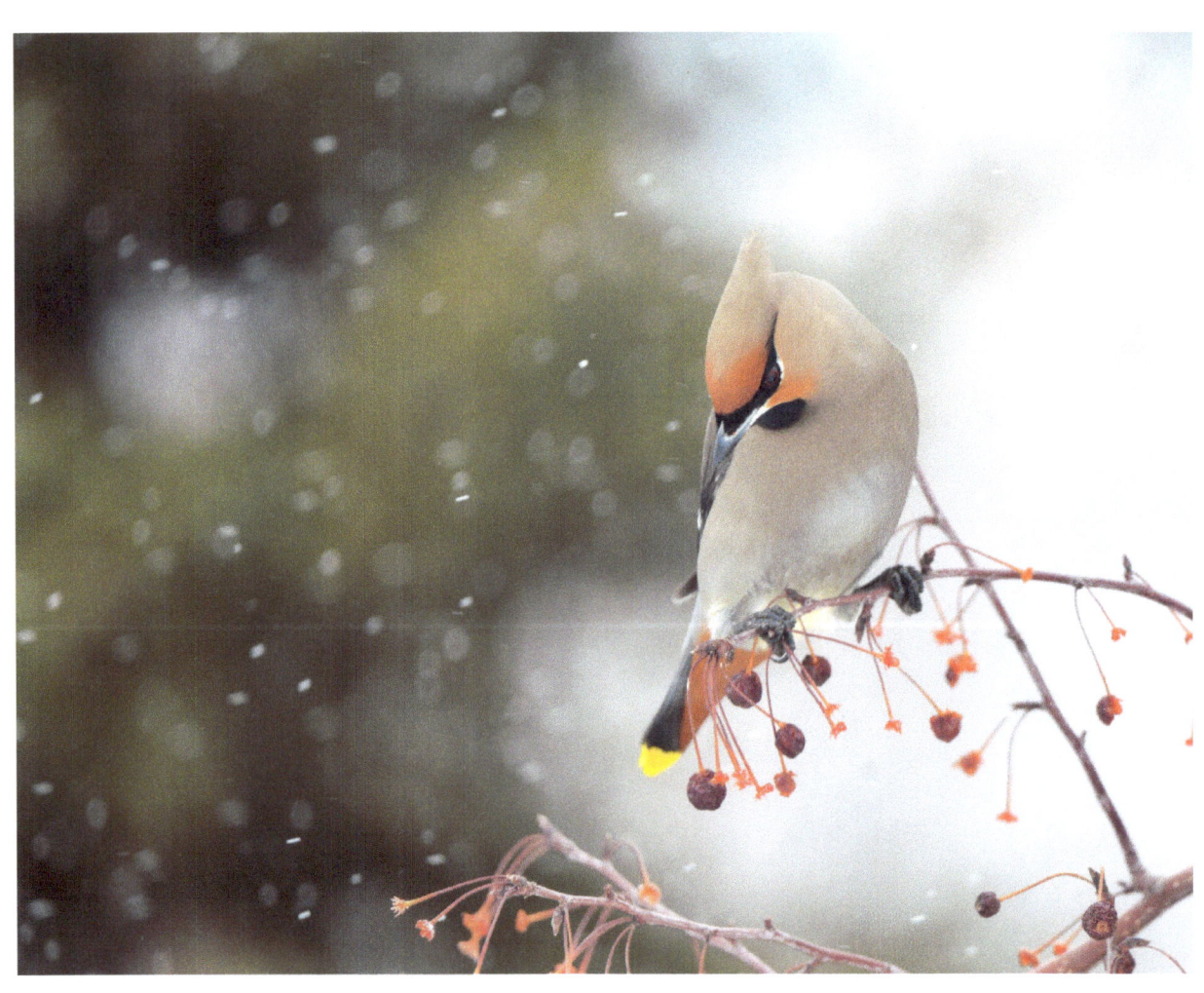

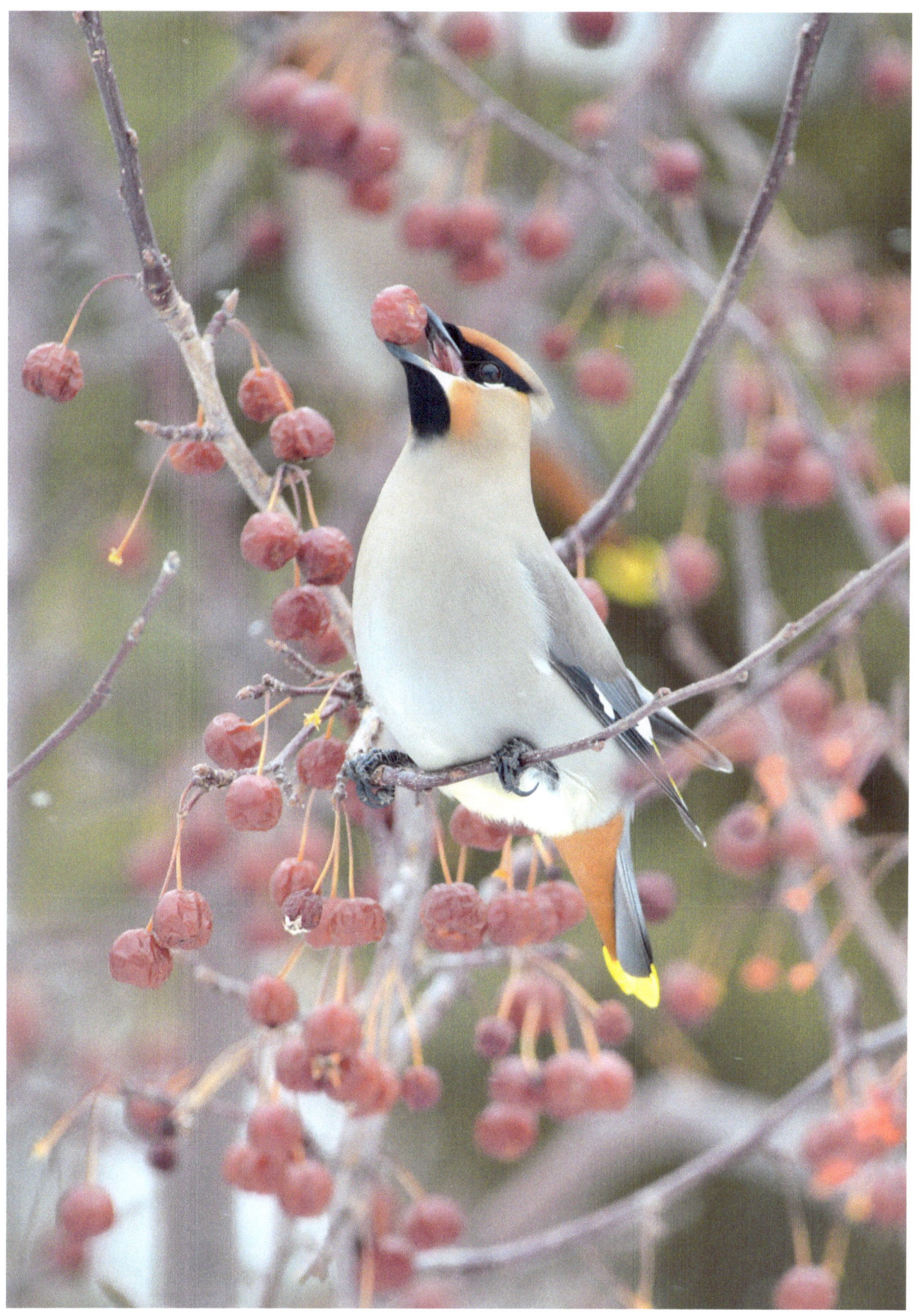

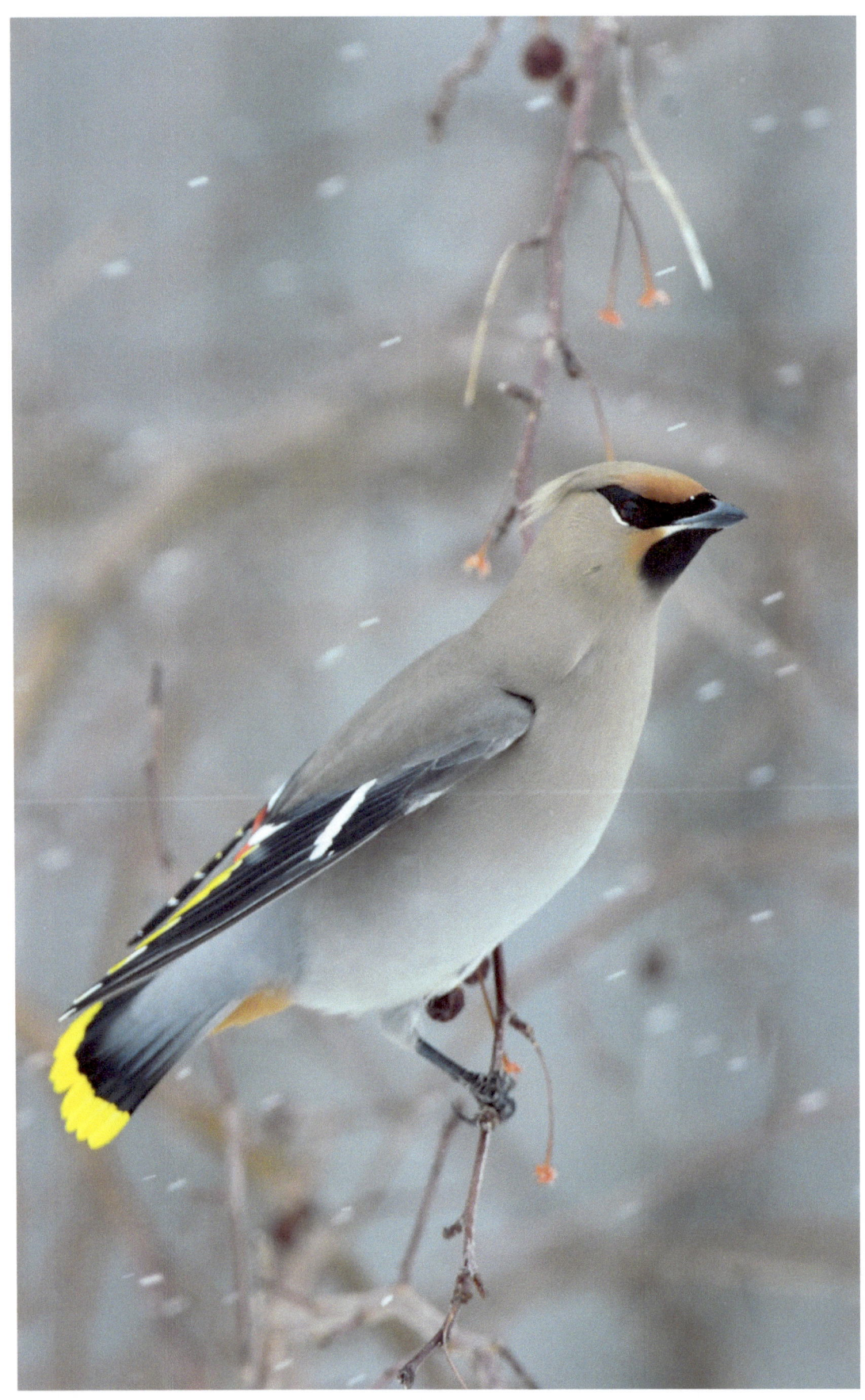

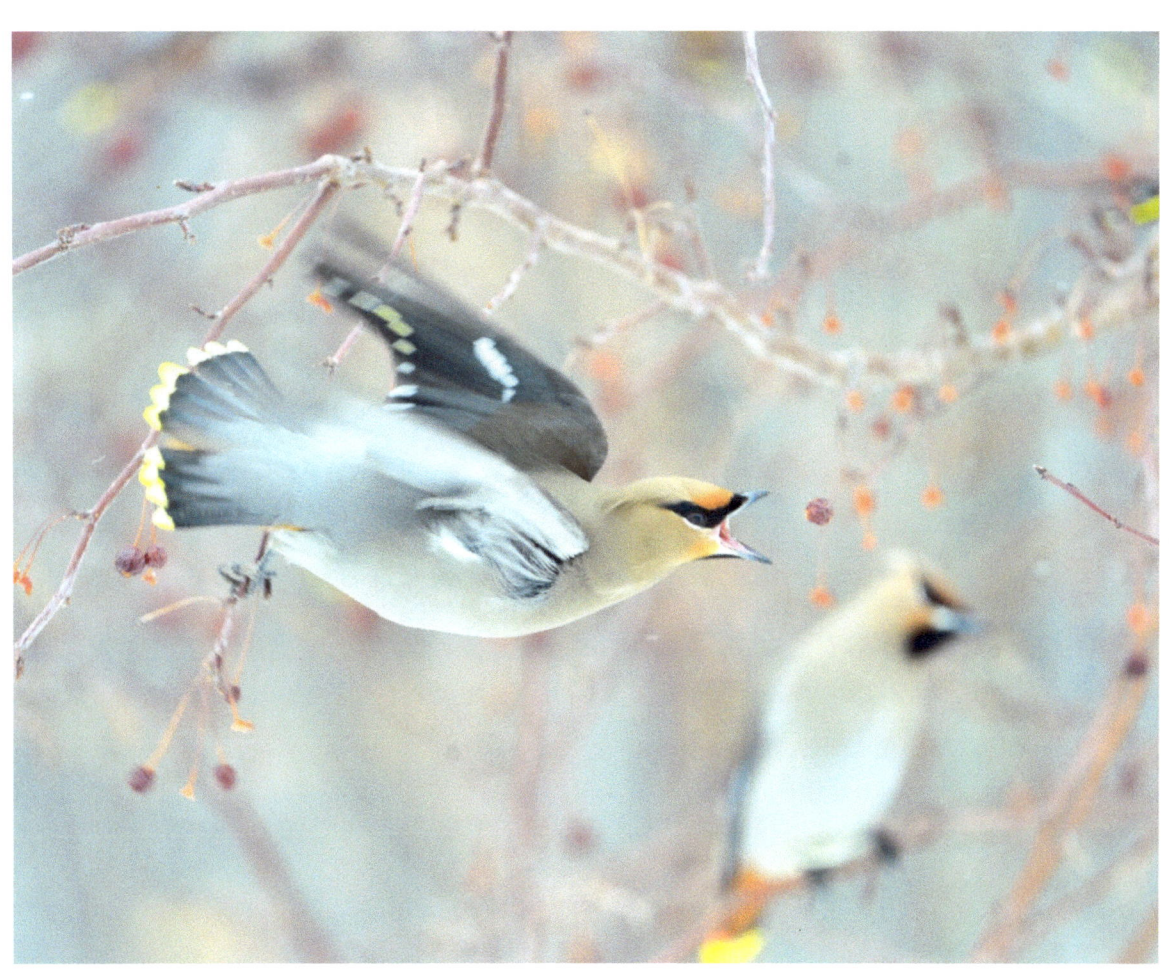

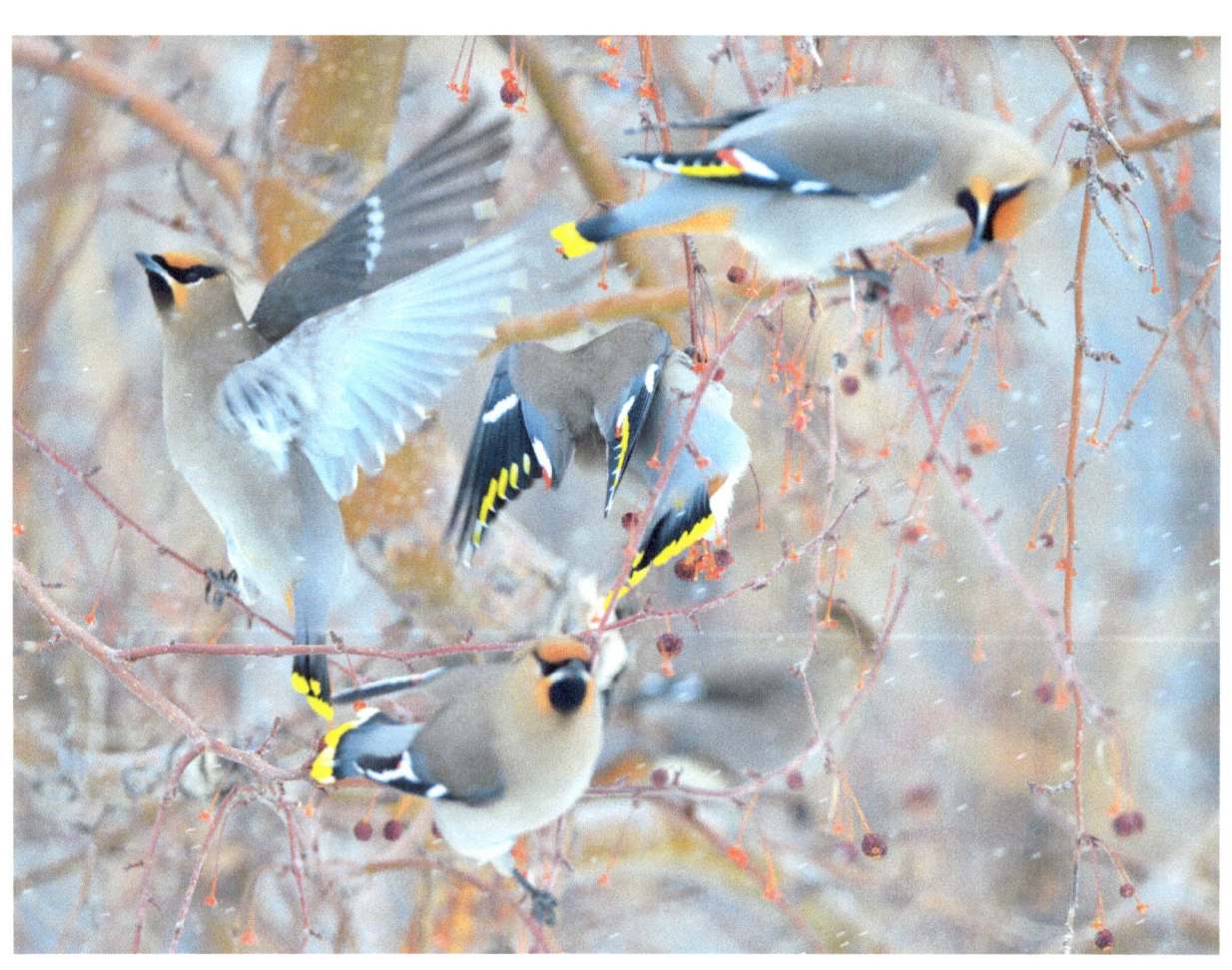

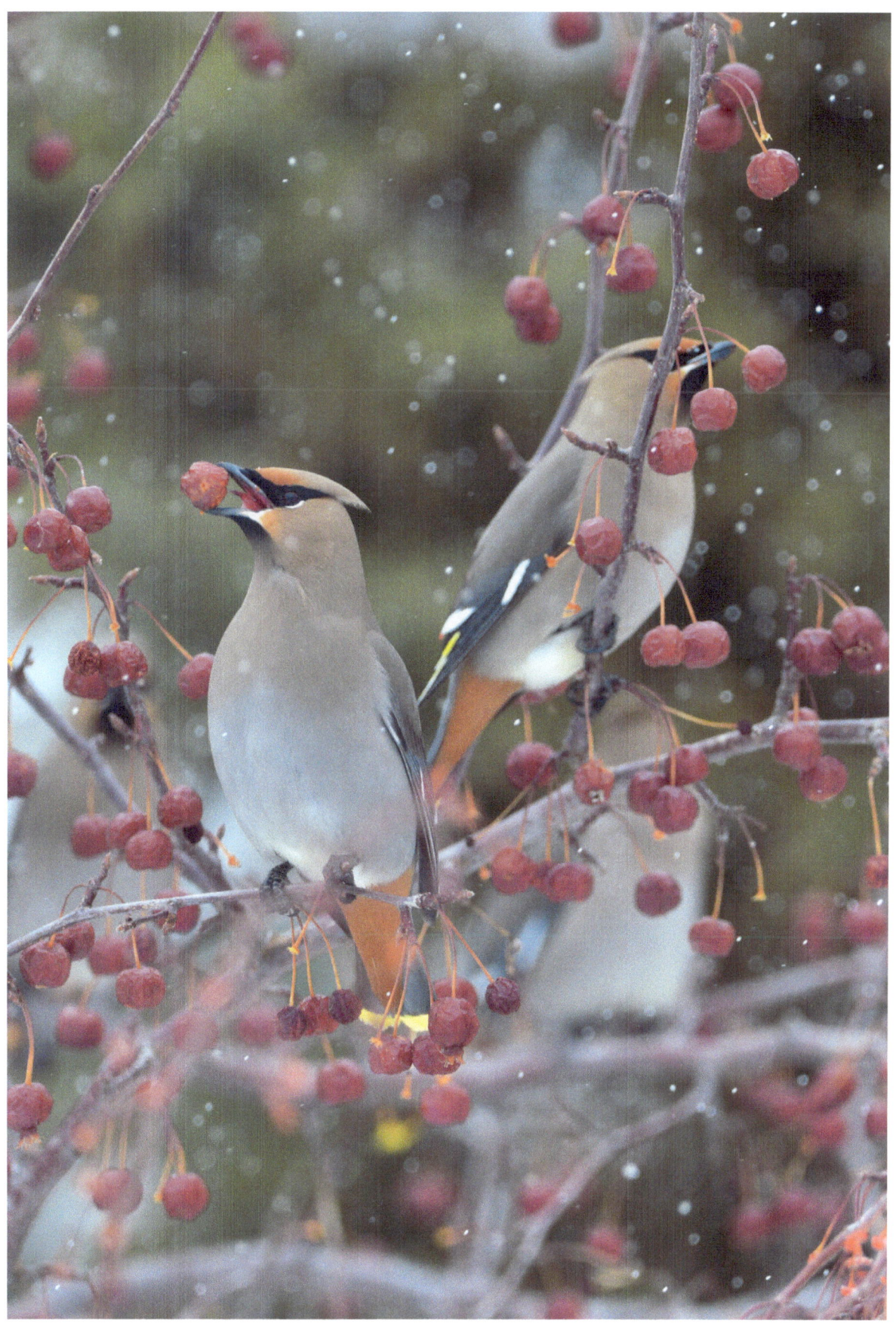

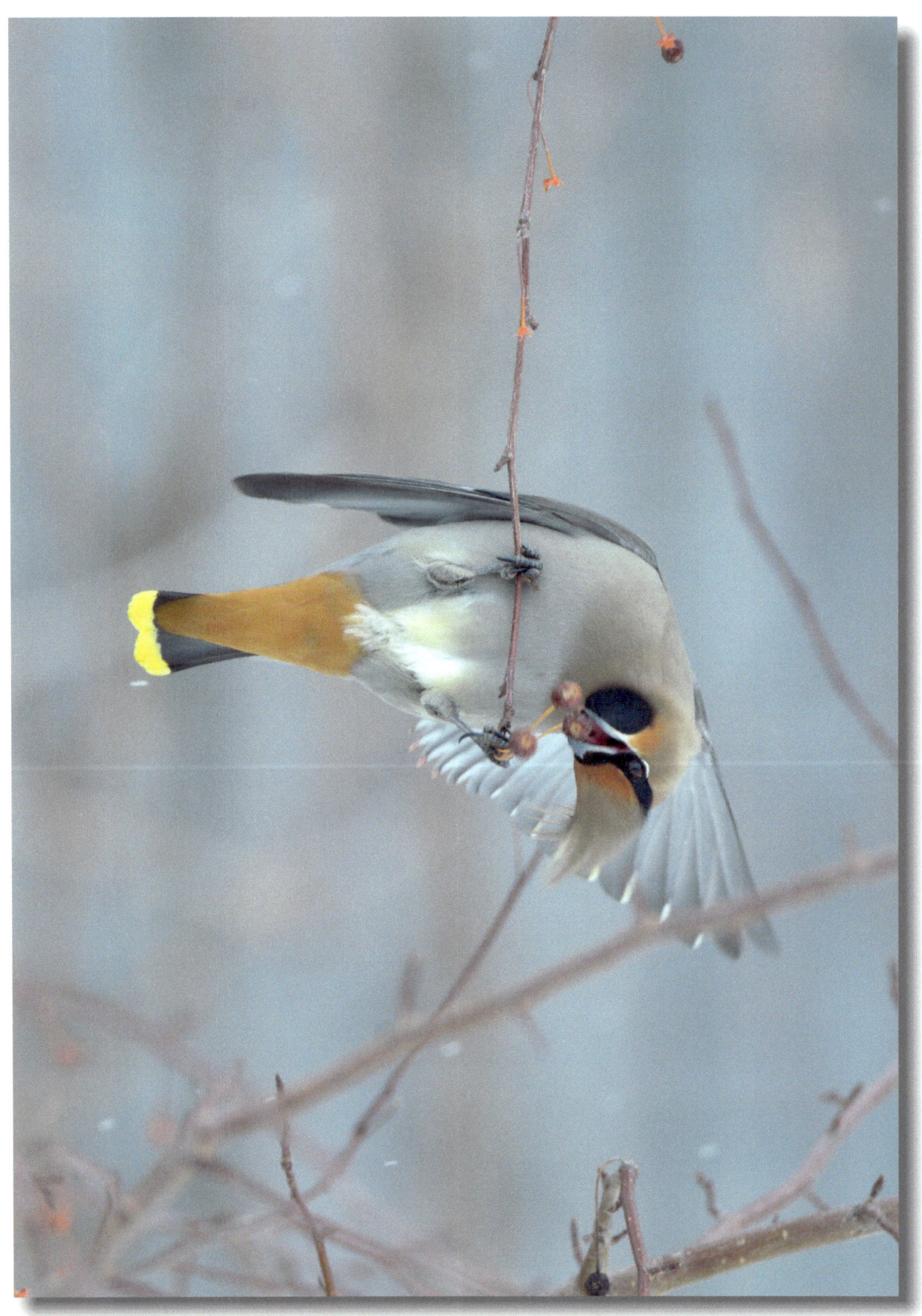

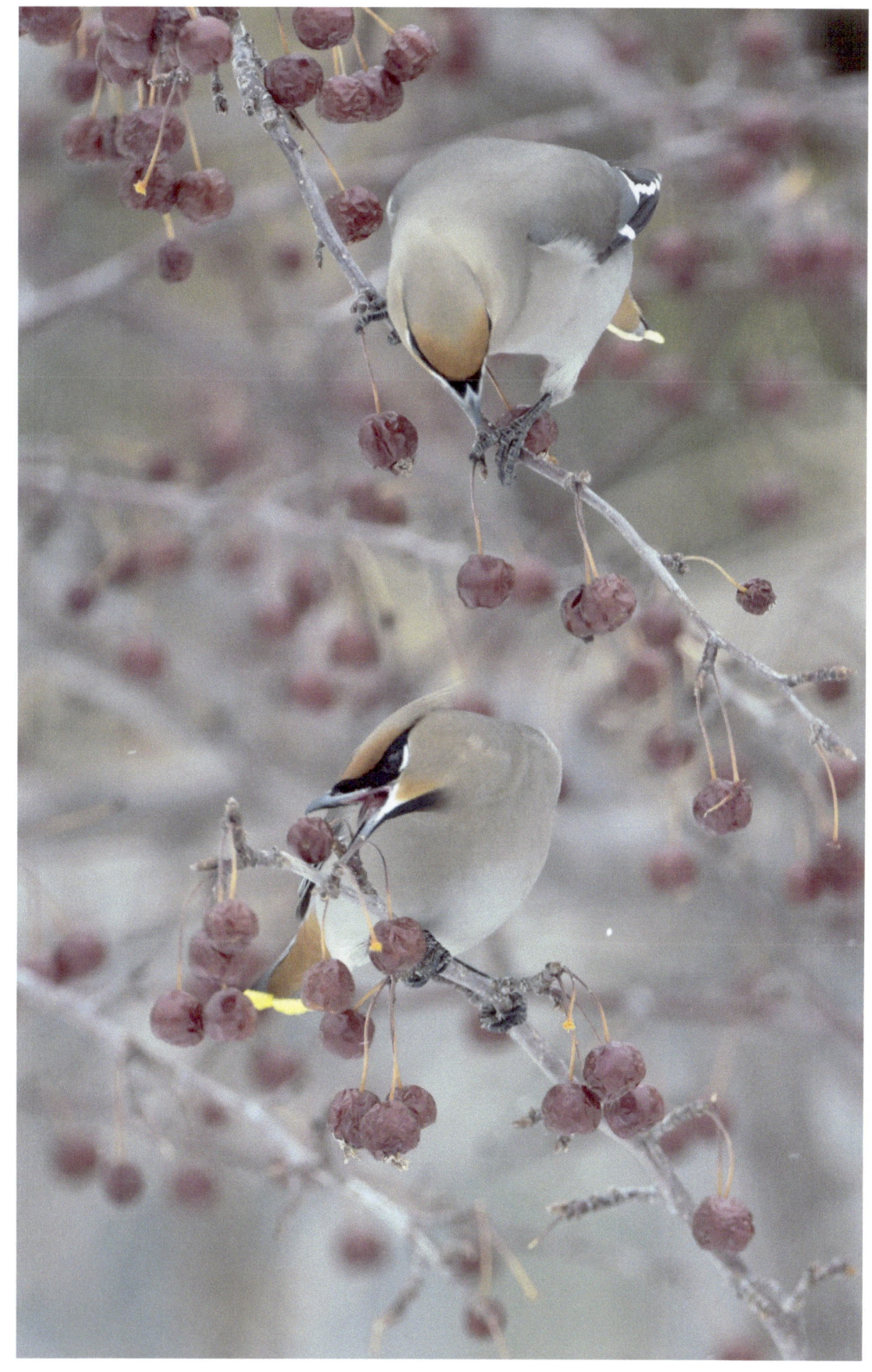

That is all for now. I wish bohemian waxwings and other migratory birds continue to pass through Saskatchewan, despite challenges of pollution, urbanization and weather changes etc.

And continue to amuse Nature lovers with their beauty.

Thanks

I acknowledge all my friends who liked my picture commented on them and provide continuous support to keep me going.

Especially Candace Savage, Peter Baran, Lennox Saunders, Deloris Burkart, Kerry Hjertaas, Catherine M Dorcas and many more.

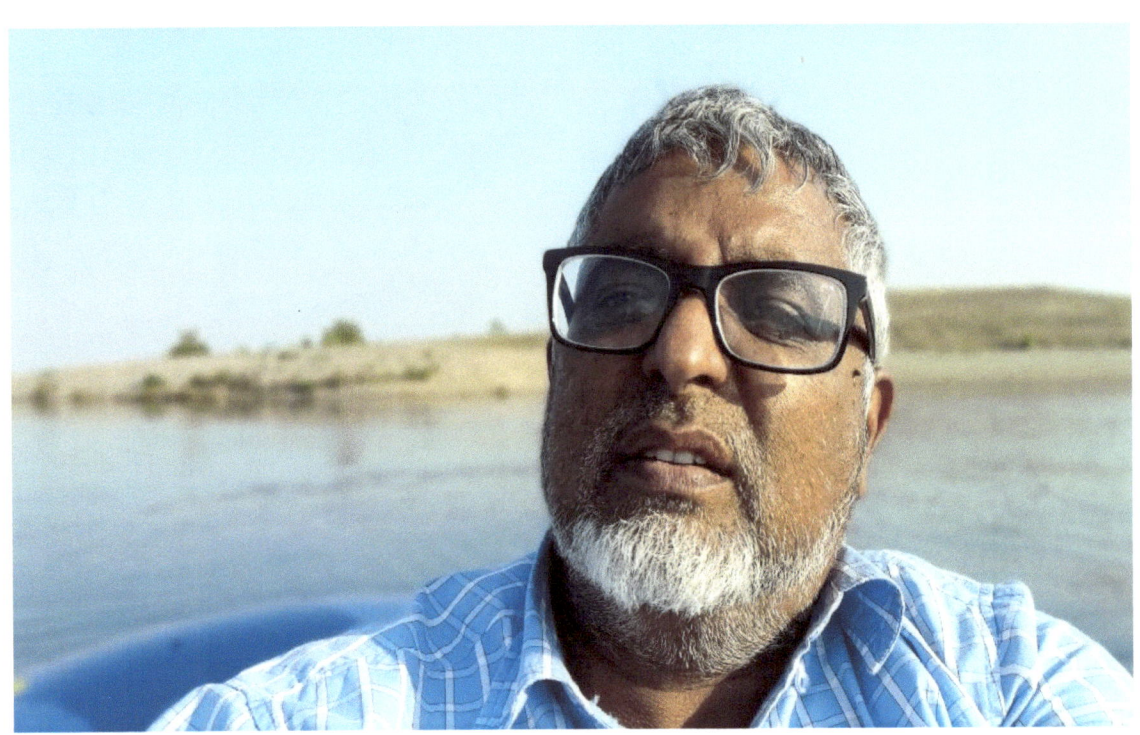

About the Author

Pervaiz Iqbal lives in Saskatoon, Saskatchewan loves nature and nature photography.

Has improved a lot in knowledge and techniques to capture nature.

Loves traveling, photography and reading.

The administrator of the Facebook page Northeast swale Nature Saskatoon.

www.ingramcontent.com/pod-product-compliance
Lightning Source LLC
Chambersburg PA
CBHW051831210526
45473CB00005B/1828